# The Passionate Sacrifice

Genesis 22

Binding Isaac

Jeffrey D. Johnson

Wipf & Stock
PUBLISHERS
Eugene, Oregon

Wipf and Stock Publishers
199 W 8th Ave, Suite 3
Eugene, OR 97401

The Passionate Sacrifice
Genesis 22: Binding Isaac
By Johnson, Jeffrey D.

ISBN 13: 978-1-55635-084-9
ISBN 10: 1-55635-084-8
Publication date 11/30/2006

# About Israel Today Ministries

*Three-fold Purpose:*

- Teach the Church about Israel
- Teach Israel about their Messiah
- Help feed those in need (Romans 15:27; Genesis 12:1-3)

To receive Dr. Johnson's "teaching letters," or, if you would like to send a gift to Israel Today Ministries, or if you would like Dr. Johnson to speak at your church event, school, or small group, contact:

**Israel Today Ministries**
**P.O. Box 150288**
**Arlington, TX 76015**
**Phone/Fax 817.468.4441**
**E mail: Galileeman@juno.com**

This is Yossef (Joseph) and Abigail. Your monthly donations help feed little ones like these.

*"Inasmuch as ye have done it unto one of the least of these my brethren, ye have done it unto me"* –Jesus, Matthew 25:40

# About Dr. Jeffrey D. Johnson

- Three decades in ministry
- Founder/Director of Israel Today Ministries
- Director of tours to the Middle East
- Senior pastor in Ohio, Massachusetts and California
- Almost 7 years directorship with International Ministries to Israel (formerly, The American Association for Jewish Evangelism, where the famed Hyman Appelman was the first president)
- Conference speaker
- Bible expositor
- Guest lecturer
- Author

Born and raised in the Midwest, Dr. Johnson took his B.D. from Massillon Baptist College, his MA from Moody Bible Institute, and his Th.M. and Th.D. from Christian Bible College. His passion for Israel, the Jewish roots of Christianity and Bible prophecy, is well known. His teaching will stir your heart to follow the Lord and to love and *"pray for the peace of Jerusalem"* (Psalm 122:6).

As an "Itinerant Bible Teacher," Dr. Johnson will travel anywhere to proclaim God's redeeming Grace through our Lord and Savior Jesus the Messiah, *"to the Jew first, and also to the Greek"* (Romans 1:16).

His call is to *"Teach the Church about Israel; Teach Israel about their Messiah; and to feed those in need"* (Genesis 12:3; Romans 15:27).

Dr. Jeff and his wife, Louise, have purposed to serve the Lord trusting God to provide the funds and resources for their livelihood.

Israel Today Ministries, founded by Dr. Johnson, is a faith ministry, supported by "love offerings" from those desiring to bless Israel. Dr. Jeff and Louise have been commissioned and sent out by their home church.

# Comments from Christian Leaders

*I am pleased to recommend him to churches as an able expositor of the Word of God.*

– *the late* **John Walvoord**, Chancellor,
Dallas Theological Seminary

*A Bible Expositor with special insights on the origin, nature and destiny of God's chosen people, Israel.*

– **John C. Whitcomb**, Bible Scholar, Author, Professor

*A careful expositor of Scripture.*

– **Homer Kent**, President Emeritus,
Grace College and Seminary

*A practitioner of all that he preaches.*

– **Paige Patterson**, former President of the
Southern Baptist Convention, President,
Southeastern Baptist Theological Seminary

*He has a wonderful grasp of Jewish history and liturgy.*

– **Edgar C. James**, Professor, Moody Bible Institute

*He is a person who has been uniquely prepared by God to preach and teach about God's special people. Any one who hears him will come away with a great love for the people of Abraham.*

–**Dick Dahlquist**, Chair, Pastoral Studies, Acting Dean,
Grace College of Graduate Studies

*He has a gifted teaching ministry which encompasses Biblical prophecy and insights into modern-day Judaism.*

–the late **Paul Tassell**, Bible Scholar, Author,
former National Representative of the G.A.R.B.C.

*He has a great ministry.*

– **LaVerne Butler**, former President of Mid-Continent Baptist College, Scholar, Conference Speaker, President, Pulpit Aflame

*Your heart will be thrilled as he ministers the prophetic Scriptures.*

– the late **Alden A. Gannett**, President Emeritus of Southeastern Bible College, Bible Scholar, Author, Conference Speaker, President, Gannett Ministries

*He loves the people and nation of Israel. He has given himself to a thorough study of God's ancient people and of the prophetic.*

– **Ivan H. French**, Pastor Emeritus, Pleasant View Bible Church, former Professor, Grace College and Seminary

## *The Preparation*

"Few narrative sections of the (Old Testament) have been subjected to as much comment and study as the 'Akedah' (or) the binding of Isaac."[1] Its subject matter ranges from the God who tests…to the man who is tested…from the nature of faith…to the demands it makes…and it considers many other questions as well…There are many levels of meaning."[2]

In this lesson, we will focus our attention on the Messianic presage it presents.

"It took the Lord (approximately) sixty years to prepare Abraham for this climactic event."[3] From the promise in Genesis 12 to the birth of Isaac in Genesis 21 was a period of 25 years. From his birth to this most salient episode was a time frame of over 30 years.

"The Lord never does put us to the test until we are ready for it."[4] There is never a testing, trial or hardship that comes our way that God has not made preparation for us to go through it. Abraham and Sarah confused and misinterpreted God's promise many times. As you reflect upon their life's story recorded in Genesis, you will find failure as well as victory. This is all part of our journey and purpose and it does not take God by surprise. Neither is the Lord ever in a hurry to accomplish that which He has started in your life. Abraham is now ready; let's look at his story.

*"And it came to pass after these things, that God did tempt Abraham, and said unto him, Abraham: and he said, Behold, here I am." Genesis 22:1*

## *Ready Lord!*

**Verse 1:** *"Here I am"* means, "ready Lord," "at your service," "yes, sir," "at once." This reflects submission. After many years he is now a yielded vessel at the feet of a holy God. Now comes the ultimate test.

*"And he said, Take now thy son, thine only son Isaac, whom thou lovest, and get thee into the land of Moriah; and offer him there for a burnt offering upon one of the mountains which I will tell thee of." Genesis 22:2*

**Verse 2:** "The original Hebrew language is far more tender than this. It should read this way: 'And he said, Take now thy son, thine only son Isaac…whom thou lovest.'"[5] "Abraham is reminded of the dearest possession of his life."[6]

The idea here is that Abraham is to do this himself…it "rules out the idea of others sharing in the test."[7] "Luther and others may not be far from the truth when he suggested that the patriarch told nothing of his purpose to Sarah."[8]

## *Your Only Son*

*"Only"* son (Hebrew, *Yachid*, "the unique one, one and only"), it has the same idea as "only begotten." Isaac was the "promised (one) child that was foretold."

"Somehow, we approach this scene with fear and trembling…we can (almost) hear God saying to us what He said to Moses… 'Take off thy shoes, for the ground whereon thou standest is holy ground.'"[9]

God says to Abraham: 'Take now your son, your only son Isaac…and offer him…on one of the mountains of which I shall tell you.' "As far as the record goes, Abraham believed God…(and) was willing to make the supreme sacrifice, to take his son and to slay him upon the altar, in order that he might please Him who called him from darkness into light."[10] That reminds us most vividly of John 3:16:

*"For God so loved the world,*
*that He gave His only begotten Son…"*

Isaiah brings a clearer focus.

*"Yet it pleased the Lord to bruise Him;*
*he hath put him to grief." Isaiah 53:10*

*"Your only son."* "What does God mean, 'your only son'? Abraham had other sons. He had Ishmael who was born thirteen years prior to Isaac. He had many sons afterward(s)…God however, recognized as a fit sacrifice only one son, the miraculously born…supernaturally given…promised son…Isaac is the only one whom God will recognize…all the blessing that will come upon the rest

of the children must come through this one particular son. God also gave His only son…but He, too, had many other sons. We read in the Book of Job about a great host of angelic beings, called the sons of God. Then, too, Adam is called by Luke, a son of God. And we, by our new creation, are the sons of God.

But angels could not fill the requirement for the substitute, and Adam could not pay for his own sin, and we…(are) unable to meet God's requirement. There was (and is) only ONE, God's only Son, who was fit to become the substitute for our sin."[11]

In Abraham we see the love of God which surpasses our understanding.

"Moriah (eight centuries later) became the site of the temple where all the sacrifices were offered …where God rent the veil in two (so) that free access might be (made) for all the people of God…."[12] This is indeed the same area in which our Lord was crucified for our sins. This is a beautiful picture (that) the Holy Spirit gives to us centuries before the Lord came.

## *Sleepless Night*

*"And Abraham rose up early in the morning, and saddled his ass, and took two of his young men with him, and Isaac his son, and clave the wood for the burnt offering, and rose up, and went unto the place of which God had told him." Genesis 22:3*

**Verse 3:** *"Early in the morning."* I don't believe Abraham slept that night. Perhaps he wrestled and agonized with

God as he did for Sodom and Gomorrah, even with greater pathos. I find an interesting parallel in the fact that our Lord, "early, (the) morning of His crucifixion, after the evening in the Passover chamber…came (to) Gethsemane."[13] The Scriptures tell us that He, Jesus, "began to be troubled and deeply distressed." (Mark 14:33) There He agonized, wrestling with His Father and praying, "Father, if it is Your will, remove this cup from Me; nevertheless not My will, but Yours, be done." (Luke 22:42)

It is appropriate that the Lord went to Gethsemane. Gethsemane means "wine press or oil press."

That fateful morning of betrayal and arrest the record tells us that Jesus "being in agony, prayed more earnestly. And His sweat became like great drops of blood falling down to the ground." (Luke 22:44) He was being "pressed", yielding to His father's will and purpose. Abraham, too….

## On the Third Day

*"Then on the third day Abraham lifted up his eyes, and saw the place afar off. And Abraham said unto his young men, Abide ye here with the ass; and I and the lad will go yonder and worship, and come again to you. And Abraham took the wood of the burnt offering, and laid it upon Isaac his son; and he took the fire in his hand, and a knife; and they went both of them together." Genesis 22:4-6*

**Verses 4-6:** *"Saw the place afar off."* "His vision included more than a mountain in the land of Moriah…. He saw past the deed to the resurrection…past the type to the fulfillment…past Isaac to the (Messiah). The New Testament will not permit any other interpretation.

*'By faith Abraham, when he was tried, offered up Isaac; and he that had received the promises offered up his only begotten son, Of whom it was said, That in Isaac shall thy seed be called: Accounting that God was able to raise him up, even from the dead...' Hebrews 11:17-19*

Our Lord reminded the Pharisees of this fact,

*'Your father Abraham rejoiced to see my day: and he saw it, and was glad.' John 8:56"*[14]

**Verse 5,6:** *"Worship"* means to "bow low, to "yield", to "submit".

*"We will come back to you."* Abraham fully believed that God would indeed raise Isaac from the dead due to the fact that God's word is true. God stated that through the promised child "all the families of the earth shall be blessed." (Genesis 12:3)

## *No Man Takes My Life*

Notice, He *"took the wood...and laid it on Isaac his son"* Abraham was 100 years older than Isaac. Isaac could easily have resisted, but did not. Here is a true picture of our Lord, who said,

*"Therefore doth my Father love me, because I lay down my life, that I might take it again. No man taketh it from me, but I lay it down of myself. I have power to lay it down, and I have power to take it again. This commandment have I received of my Father." John 10:17,18*

"Abraham would have been no match for Isaac, if he had resisted...but Isaac bore the wood, as Christ bore the cross."[15]

*"Fire and knife."* As the wood points to the cross, "Fire in the Scripture has the meaning of judgment. Again and again fire and flame speak of judgment in preparation for the love of God. It was a flame and a sword that guarded Eden.... It was fire which destroyed Sodom and Gomorrah...and very significantly the place of eternal judgment is called the lake of fire. We have here then a picture of the Cross and the judgment which was to fall upon another Son because of the sin of humanity."[16]

"Knife", a butcher knife, a sacrificial knife, used in sacrificing animals. "A knife in Scripture speaks of the Word of God."[17]

*"For the word of God is quick, and powerful, and sharper than any two-edged sword..." Hebrews 4:12*

"God foreknew and foresaw that man would sin. Even before man was created, God had ready a plan of salvation which included the death of His Son. John in Revelation tells us that Jesus is the 'Lamb slain from before the foundation of the world.' (Revelation 13:8) You see, (Jesus) came in the fulness of time, according to the promise and according to the Word of God, with a knife in His hand."[18]

*"Two of them went together."* "The narrative gives free play to our imagination as it pictures (the) father and son proceeding step (by) step up the hill."[19] "Here we have perfect agreement. Abraham did not have to force his son to climb up....They were both agreed and of one mind...."[20] The son was obedient unto death.

*"...He is brought as a lamb to the slaughter, and as a sheep before her shearers is dumb, so he openeth not his mouth." Isaiah 53:7*

*"And Isaac spake unto Abraham his father, and said, My father: and he said, Here am I, my son. And he said, Behold the fire and the wood: but where is the lamb for a burnt offering? And Abraham said, My son, God will provide himself a lamb for a burnt offering: so they went both of them together." Genesis 22:7,8*

## *Where is the Lamb?*

**Verses 7,8:** The two of them went together. But Isaac spoke...

The idea is that the father and son walked in oppressive silence...until Isaac asked the question, "Where is the lamb, Father?" Isaac knew what was necessary for sacrifice. Abraham's response is full of pathos. The question pierced Abraham's heart like a knife. Trembling with great apprehension he said, "Behold me, my son," or, "Yes, my son." "Here am I, my son."

"God will provide for Himself the lamb." *Jehovah-Jireh, 'the Lord will see to it', 'provide', 'look out for' or 'choose.'* The Lord will provide....

*"My son"* is an expression of tenderness. As though Abraham was sparing Isaac from unnecessary pain and detail. Abraham fully intended to sacrifice his son...To spill his blood, to burn his body. He did not know there would be a ram in the bushes. He leaves this painful issue with a merciful God. Abraham's presage was nothing less than profound. "The Lord will see to it." "The Lord will provide." *"The Lord will provide Himself..."* He knew that "(God)

Himself is going to pay the price...He Himself is going to be the Lamb in the person of His Son. What a marvelous truth of the atonement! When no one else could pay, God said, 'I'll pay the price.' That answer satisfied Isaac... 'and the two of them went together.'"[21]

## *Sleep-Walking*

*"And they came to the place which God had told him of; and Abraham built an altar there, and laid the wood in order, and bound Isaac his son, and laid him on the altar upon the wood. And Abraham stretched forth his hand, and took the knife to slay his son." Genesis 22:9,10*

**Verses 9,10:** Notice "the staccato phrases that heighten the tension. (The short, abrupt, pithy statements).... Abraham seems to move 'like a sleep-walker.'"[22] (being numb, or receiving bad news, death) Abraham actually binds his son. Isaac submits to this act in total otherworldly confidence in his father. "A confidence built upon a complete understanding and a deep love which knew that the father could wish his son no harm."[23]

"In Leviticus, where the continuing sacrifices are begun, we discover that the pieces of wood were laid in order upon the altar (Leviticus 1:7), and that a horizontal bolt of fire from the Holy of Holies ignited the wood and consumed the offering (Leviticus 9:24). God Himself furnished the material and the fire (that) consumed the sacrifice, for He Himself (will) put His Son to death (Isaiah 53:10)... 'it pleased the Lord to bruise Him...'"[24]

## *The Sacred Moment*

**Verse 10:** "The center of the scene shifts from the father to son and back to the father, for the Lord is emphasizing the fact that both were going to the sacrifice together, obeying, yielding, co-operating even as the heavenly Father and the Lord Jesus Christ did at Calvary. With the consent of Isaac, Abraham binds him…and lays him on the altar…."[25]

Another important point is that …on top of the mountain…there was no one around except Abraham and Isaac. "When they went to the place of sacrifice, they took two men along…but when they came to the mountain, Abraham said, 'You two stay behind….' When that awful moment came…Abraham lifted up his…(knife)…there was no one around, no one to witness it, no one to see it…(WHY?) The scene was too sacred, too holy…Do you see the picture?

When the Son of God went up to Calvary, His father went with Him, and was right there at Calvary, holding His Son's hand as He walked up the mountain…. But there were two other men also, one on the right hand, and one on the left…. (Then) the time came for the sacrifice, the time for that holy scene which no eye might behold. Just as Abraham denied the two men who went with them an opportunity to see the actual transaction, so also did God…. (You see) for when the time came, every one must be shut out, and no one must see. From the sixth hour 'there was darkness over the whole earth until the ninth hour.' (Matthew 27:45) For three hours no human eye beheld what took place on the Cross of Calvary. The Father snuffed out the lights of heaven, He pulled down the shades of the sky, separated Himself with His Son alone."[26]

"At the end of those three black hours we hear a cry, as the Father seems to say to His son, 'I've got to go now.... The rest of the way you will have to go all alone...by yourself... all alone.' And (then) there comes the piercing cry from the Son of God upon the Cross, (Eli, Eli, Lama Sabachthani) 'My God, My God, why hast thou forsaken me?' Alone He had to die and pay the price, so that you and I would never have to be alone...so that we would never have to experience the loneliness of being forever forsaken."[27] At that very moment He bore our sin.

## *Isaac Died*

*"And the angel of the Lord called unto him out of heaven, and said, Abraham, Abraham: and he said, Here am I. And he said, Lay not thine hand upon the lad, neither do thou any thing unto him: for now I know that thou fearest God, seeing thou hast not withheld thy son, thine only son from me. And Abraham lifted up his eyes, and looked, and behold behind him a ram caught in a thicket by his horns: and Abraham went and took the ram, and offered him up for a burnt offering in the stead of his son." Genesis 22:11-13*

**Verses 11-13:** The record states that Isaac died...

*"By faith Abraham, when he was tried, OFFERED UP Isaac; and he that had received the promises OFFERED UP his ONLY BEGOTTEN SON," Hebrews 11:17*

*"Accounting that God was able to RAISE HIM UP... from the DEAD..." Hebrews 11:19*

"How long was Isaac dead? Three days...exactly three days...Abraham actually offered up his son in the sight of

God…as far as Abraham was concerned, Isaac was really dead. When Abraham started out on the journey early…that morning…he had no other idea…than that…God meant what He said…and that he must after three days put Isaac to death on Mt. Moriah. For three days he considered his son, Isaac, dead, potentially dead…Isaac had been dead in the mind of Abraham for three days and now all of a sudden he is returned to life."[28]

What a wonderful picture that after three days Isaac was raised from the dead…. Abraham knew the joy of resurrection "upon the (very) mountain where the Son of God was to be slain."[29]

"Abraham believed in the death and the resurrection of his son."[30] Abraham believed the gospel, (the death, burial and resurrection) and was a child of God. Paul referred to this when he stated,

*"And the Scripture, foreseeing that God would justify the heathen by faith, preached before the gospel unto Abraham, saying, 'In thee shall all nations be blessed.'" Galatians 3:8*

## *The Ram*

The ram is a picture of our Lord becoming our substitute, paying the ultimate price for our sins. The ram has played a significant role throughout biblical history. "Its skin provided a mantle for Elijah…(it was used to make) the strings of David's harp…and its two horns…the two trumpets: one to be sounded later at the great revelation of God at Mount Sinai…and the other to be blown at…the coming of the Messiah (Last Trump)." [31]

*"And Abraham called the name of that place Jehovah- Jireh: as it is said to this day, In the mount of the Lord it shall be seen." Genesis 22:14*

**Verse 14:** *Jehovah-Jireh,* the Lord will provide…the Lord will see to it. "In the Mount of the Lord it shall be provided"…. "Should be translated, 'In the mount the Lord shall be seen.'"[32]

"Isaac is a type of the Lord Jesus Christ up to a certain point, and then the ram takes his place and becomes God's provision for the sinner. Abraham understood all the meaning of these things. We hear Jesus saying in John 8:56,

*'Your father Abraham rejoiced to see my day:*
*and he saw it, and was glad.'"* [33]

## *Climbing Your Mountain*

Question: Have you climbed this mountain in your life? This Mt. Moriah? Christian, have you been to this mountain…the mountain of struggling to know God's will? Take comfort in Abraham's faith in the unknown. He did not know exactly how this was going to unfold. He only knew that God is true to His word…in that Isaac was the promised child…and that God told him to go to the mountain.

"Often, followers of God wonder how they may know the will of God. Ninety per cent of the knowing of the will of God consists in your willingness to do it before it is (completely) known (I and the lad will go up yonder and 'worship'), when we are ready to pick up the knife…or…to lay it down, God will pour out His richest blessing(s)."[34]

"Faith may be timid when it has not been fully tested… and although we are never to trust in previous triumphs… but in God alone…those triumphs are there as landmarks of the trustworthiness of God."[35]

Look back in your life…do you see the landmarks? Are you being tested? Are you going through an unbearable trial?

Remember…Jehovah-Jireh, God will provide…He will see to it…God is faithful. Even "if we are faithless, He remains faithful." (2 Timothy 2:13)

Now let me speak to the non-Christian, the seeker, the non-believer for a moment. Will you climb this mountain of faith? Believing on the Lord, trusting in Him alone? Will you repent, turning away from sin and turn to the Cross? The Scriptures state,

*"But God commendeth his love toward us, in that, while we were yet sinners, Christ died for us." Romans 5:8*

This is what this lesson is about. The substitute…the Lamb of God…who takes away our sin when we trust in Him alone. Will you trust Him? Will you come to the foot of the mountain called Mt. Calvary and embrace the Cross?

*"For God so loved the world that He gave…"*

He provided. He loves you. Oh, how He loves you...

## *Endnotes*

[1] W. Gunther Plaut, *"The Torah, A Modern Commentary, Genesis"*, (The Union of American Hebrew Congregations, New York, 1974), p. 203.
[2] Ibid., p. 203.
[3] M.R. DeHaan, *"Adventures in Faith, Studies in the Life of Abraham,"* (Zondervan Publishing House, Grand Rapids, 1953), p. 153.
[4] Ibid., p. 153.
[5] Ibid., p. 156.
[6] W.H. Griffith Thomas, D.D., *"Genesis, A Devotional Commentary"*, (Eerdmans Publishing, Grand Rapids, 1946), p. 195.
[7] H.C. Leupold, D.D., *"Exposition of Genesis, Volume II"*, (Baker Book House, Grand Rapids, 1964), p. 620.
[8] Ibid., p. 620.
[9] M.R. DeHaan, *"Adventures in Faith, Studies in the Life of Abraham"*, (Zondervan Publishing House, Grand Rapids, 1953), p. 156.
[10] Ibid., pp. 156,157.
[11] Ibid., pp. 157,158.
[12] Donald Grey Barnhouse, *"Genesis, A Devotional Exposition"*, (Zondervan Publishing House, Grand Rapids, 1973), p. 197.
[13] M.R. DeHaan, *"Adventures in Faith, Studies in the Life of Abraham"*, (Zondervan Publishing House, Grand Rapids, 1953), p. 160.
[14] Donald Grey Barnhouse, *"Genesis, A Devotional Exposition"*, (Zondervan Publishing House, Grand Rapids, 1973), p. 199.
[15] Ibid., p. 200.
[16] M.R. DeHaan, *"Adventures in Faith, Studies in the Life of Abraham"*, (Zondervan Publishing House, Grand Rapids, 1953), p. 162.
[17] Ibid., p. 162.
[18] Ibid., p. 162.
[19] H.C. Leupold, D.D., *"Exposition of Genesis, Volume II"*, (Baker Book House, Grand Rapids, 1964), p. 625.
[20] M.R. DeHaan, *"Adventures in Faith, Studies in the Life of Abraham"*, (Zondervan Publishing House, Grand Rapids, 1953), p. 162.
[21] Ibid., p. 164.
[22] W. Gunther Plaut, *"The Torah, A Modern Commentary, Genesis"*, (The Union of American Hebrew Congregations, New York, 1974), p. 206.
[23] H.C. Leupold, D.D., *"Exposition of Genesis, Volume II"*, (Baker Book House, Grand Rapids, 1964), p. 627.
[24] Donald Grey Barnhouse, *"Genesis, A Devotional Exposition"*, (Zondervan Publishing House, Grand Rapids, 1973), p. 201.

[25] Ibid., p. 202.
[26] M.R. DeHaan, *"Adventures in Faith, Studies in the Life of Abraham"*, (Zondervan Publishing House, Grand Rapids, 1953), p. 164-165.
[27] Ibid., p. 165.
[28] Ibid. p. 166.
[29] Ibid. p. 167.
[30] Ibid., p. 167.
[31] David Goldstein, *"Jewish Legends"*, (Peter Bedrick books, New York, 1987), pp. 57,58.
[32] Donald Grey Barnhouse, *"Genesis, A Devotional Exposition"*, (Zondervan Publishing House, Grand Rapids, 1973), p. 204.
[33] M.R. DeHaan, *"Adventures in Faith, Studies in the Life of Abraham"*, (Zondervan Publishing House, Grand Rapids, 1953), p. 168-169.
[34] Donald Grey Barnhouse, *"Genesis, A Devotional Exposition"*, (Zondervan Publishing House, Grand Rapids, 1973), p. 202.
[35] Ibid., p. 203.